# The Tigris and Euphrates

## Rivers of the Fertile Crescent

By Gary Miller

CRABTREE
Publishing Company
www.crabtreebooks.com

# Crabtree Publishing Company

www.crabtreebooks.com

**Author**: Gary Miller
**Editor**: Barbara Bakowski
**Designer**: Tammy West, Westgraphix LLC
**Photo Researcher**: Edward A. Thomas
**Map Illustrator**: Stefan Chabluk
**Indexer**: Nila Glikin
**Project Coordinator**: Kathy Middleton
**Crabtree Editor**: Adrianna Morganelli
**Proofreader**: Reagan Miller
**Production Coordinator**: Kenneth Wright
**Prepress Technician**: Kenneth Wright

**Series Consultant**: Michael E. Ritter, Ph.D., Professor of Geography, University of Wisconsin—Stevens Point

Developed for Crabtree Publishing Company by RJF Publishing LLC (www.RJFpublishing.com)

**Cover**: Small boats on the water near Al Qurnah, Iraq, where the Tigris and Euphrates rivers meet to form the Shatt al Arab.

**Photo Credits**:
Cover: Goster Glase/Superstock/Photolibrary
4, 12: © Nik Wheeler/CORBIS
6, 18: (bottom) Getty Images
7: AFP/Getty Images
8: © Images & Stories/Alamy
10: © Trip/Alamy
13, 17: iStockphoto
14: © North Wind/North Wind Picture Archives-all rights reserved
18: (top) Suleiman I (1494-1566) called the"Magnificent" (gouache on paper) by Italian school (16thcentury)/ Bibliotheque Nationale,Paris,France/Archives Charmet/ The Bridgeman Art Library
19: Popperfoto/Getty Images
20: © Chad McDermott/Alamy
21: ATEF HASSAN/Reuters/Landov
23, 24: AP Images
25: Michele Burgess/Superstock/Photolibrary
27: Reuters/Landov

**Library and Archives Canada Cataloguing in Publication**

Miller, Gary, 1961-
   The Tigris and Euphrates : rivers of the fertile crescent / Gary G. Miller.

(Rivers around the world)
Includes index.
ISBN 978-0-7787-7448-8 (bound).--ISBN 978-0-7787-7471-6 (pbk.)

   1. Tigris River--Juvenile literature. 2. Tigris River Valley--Juvenile literature. 3. Euphrates River--Juvenile literature. 4. Euphrates River Valley--Juvenile literature. I. Title. II. Series: Rivers around the world

DS49.7.M54 2010          j956.7          C2009-906244-5

**Library of Congress Cataloging-in-Publication Data**

Miller, Gary, 1961-
 The Tigris and Euphrates : rivers of the fertile crescent / by Gary Miller.
       p. cm. --  (Rivers around the world)
 Includes index.
 ISBN 978-0-7787-7471-6 (pbk. : alk. paper) -- ISBN 978-0-7787-7448-8 (reinforced library binding : alk. paper)
1.  Tigris River--Juvenile literature. 2.  Tigris River Valley--Juvenile literature. 3.  Euphrates River--Juvenile literature. 4.  Euphrates River Valley--Juvenile literature.  I. Title. II. Series.

 DS49.7.M55 2009
 956.7--dc22

                                    2009042411

**Crabtree Publishing Company**
www.crabtreebooks.com     1-800-387-7650

Printed in the U.S.A./032014/JA20140203

**Published in Canada**
**Crabtree Publishing**
616 Welland Ave.
St. Catharines, ON
L2M 5V6

**Published in the United States**
**Crabtree Publishing**
PMB 59051
350 Fifth Avenue, 59th Floor
New York, New York 10118

**Published in the United Kingdom**
**Crabtree Publishing**
Maritime House
Basin Road North, Hove
BN41 1WR

**Published in Australia**
**Crabtree Publishing**
386 Mt. Alexander Rd.
Ascot Vale (Melbourne)
VIC 3032

# CONTENTS

Words that are defined in the glossary are in **bold** type
the first time they appear in the text.

# CHAPTER 1

# Between the Rivers

At nine o'clock in the morning, the temperature is already a scorching 100 degrees Fahrenheit (38 degrees Celsius). Desert stretches for miles around, yet just ahead is a lush field of crops. How is this possible? You are in the Tigris-Euphrates river basin, one of the most unusual environments on Earth.

The Tigris and Euphrates rivers begin in the mountains of Turkey and follow separate courses until they join to become the Shatt al Arab near the Persian Gulf.

## Follow the Flow

The Tigris and Euphrates rivers flow from rugged mountains in Turkey, where rain and melting snow feed them. The Tigris flows about 1,180 miles (1,900 kilometers) before joining the Euphrates River in Iraq. The Euphrates flows 1,740 miles (2,800 km) before it combines with the Tigris to form the Shatt al Arab, which empties into the Persian Gulf.

The Tigris-Euphrates **drainage basin**, or the area of land that is drained by the rivers, covers about 475,865 square miles (765,830 square km). Much of the land through which the rivers flow is desert. Water from the rivers makes it possible for people to live in this hot, arid environment.

## The Land of Mesopotamia

People have lived in the Tigris and Euphrates basin since about 10,000 BC. The first settlers lived in a place

LEFT: The Kara Su River in northeastern Turkey is a source of the Euphrates River.

**FAST FACT**
The Sumerian name for the Tigris River was Idigna, or "fast water."

The Tigris River flows through Baghdad, the capital of Iraq.

known as Mesopotamia. The name *Mesopotamia* comes from Greek words meaning "land between the rivers." The land near the Tigris and Euphrates was home to a number of rich cultures, including the ancient kingdoms of Sumer, Babylonia, Akkad, and Assyria. It was also part of the **Fertile Crescent**, a landscape of rivers and rich soil that extended from the eastern shore of the Mediterranean Sea to the Persian Gulf.

## An Important Resource

The Tigris and Euphrates rivers provided vital resources for early people. Most important was water, which people used for drinking and crop **irrigation**. The rivers flooded regularly, depositing nutrient-rich **silt** on the land, which helped crops grow well. People caught fish in the rivers and hunted birds and other animals that lived along the shores. Early settlers also used the rivers as an important route for travel and trade.

Today, millions of people live in the Tigris and Euphrates basin. Many live in large cities that have developed along the rivers, such as Baghdad, in Iraq. Outside the cities, farmers grow crops, including sugar beets, olives, and grains. Herders raise goats, cattle, and other livestock. Water from the Tigris and Euphrates rivers remains a critical resource.

NOTABLE QUOTE

*"Marduk created…and put in place Tigris and Euphrates rivers. He pronounced their names with favor."*

—from the Babylonian creation myth "Marduk the Creator"

This photograph shows people attending the opening of a new irrigation canal on the Tigris River that will carry water for agriculture.

## Putting Water to Work

To bring water to crops, people along the Tigris and Euphrates rivers have built complex irrigation systems. Dams capture water that flows down the rivers. **Canals** and pumps deliver the water to places where it is needed.

## That's Electric!

How does a river help create electrical power? A dam captures water flowing down a river. The water is held behind the dam, forming a **reservoir**, or an artificial lake. When the water is released through a channel, the moving water spins the blades of a giant **turbine**. The turbine is connected to a **generator**, which makes electricity as it turns.

Dams also serve another important function: they use the force of moving water to generate **hydroelectricity**.

## Sharing the Rivers

The need for water in the region of the Tigris and Euphrates has created conflicts. Since the 1960s, Turkey, Syria, and Iraq have worked to share the river waters in ways that are fair to people in all the countries located within the basin. The nations have often disagreed about how the water should be shared, however.

As the population along the Tigris and Euphrates rivers has increased, the demand for water has grown, too. Another problem is that a change in weather patterns may be bringing less rain and snow to the river basin. Today, the Tigris and Euphrates rivers are pushed to their limits, yet people across the region are hopeful that the rivers will continue to provide the water they need.

# CHAPTER 2

# From the Mountains to the Gulf

The Tigris and Euphrates rivers start within 50 miles (80 km) of each other, high in the mountains of Turkey. As they flow along separate courses until they meet near the Persian Gulf, the rivers pass through the region that was a birthplace of civilization thousands of years ago—Mesopotamia.

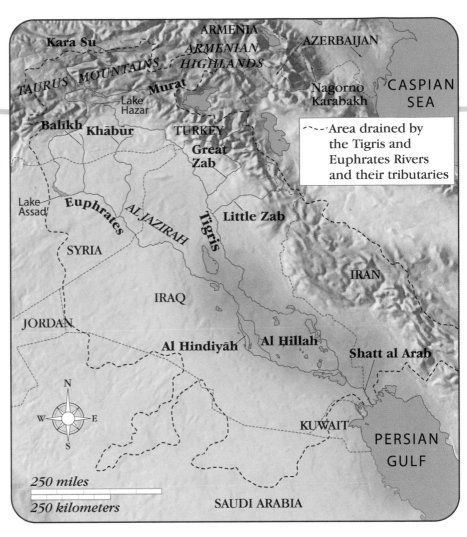

Turkey, Syria, and Iraq share the Tigris-Euphrates basin—and sometimes experience conflict over the rivers' waters.

## The Tigris

The source of the Tigris River is Lake Hazar, located in the Taurus Mountains of eastern Turkey. Beyond Lake Hazar, the Tigris River drops swiftly through a series of rocky **gorges** and steep-walled valleys until it reaches the highlands of Syria.

The Tigris River flows along the border between Turkey and Syria and enters Iraq. Near the Iraqi city of Mosul, the river is joined by two major **tributaries**, the Great Zab and the Little Zab rivers.

Near the town of Sāmarrā, the Tigris enters Iraq's **alluvial plain**. An alluvial plain is a flat area of land created over time by the deposit of sediment by a river or rivers. At Baghdad, Iraq's capital, artificial **embankments** help keep the river from flooding. An embankment is a raised structure, often of earth or gravel, used to hold back water. The Tigris River joins the Euphrates River about 120 miles (190 km) northwest of the Persian Gulf.

## The Euphrates

The Euphrates River has two river sources, the Murat and the Kara Su. They begin in the Armenian Highlands of northeastern Turkey. The Murat and Kara Su join at Keban, forming the Euphrates River. The Keban Dam, completed in 1974, created a large reservoir.

LEFT: The Tigris River flows through a deep gorge in the Taurus Mountains of Turkey.

A Madan, or Marsh Arab, travels by boat through the wetlands of southern Iraq.

After exiting the dam, the Euphrates River drops to the plains of southeastern Turkey. It flows southwest to within about 100 miles (160 km) of the Mediterranean Sea and then turns southward and enters Syria. Near the city of Ar Raqqah is the Lake Assad reservoir. It was created by the Euphrates Dam, which was built in 1973. Below the dam, two major tributaries, the Balīkh and Khābūr rivers, enter the Euphrates.

After entering Iraq, the Euphrates River flows toward the city of Al Fallūjah, where the river enters the alluvial plain. There the river slows and eventually divides into two branches, Al Hindiyāh and Al Hillah. The Al Hindiyāh Barrage, built in 1914,

## An "Island" Between Rivers

Between the Tigris and Euphrates rivers is a limestone **plateau**, or level uplifted area, called the Al Jazīrah. The Arabic name means "island." Here the Tigris and Euphrates rivers run in **limestone** channels that have changed little over thousands of years.

**FAST FACT**
The name *Shatt al Arab* means "stream of the Arabs." This river was named for the people who live along it.

al Arab. So do the tides in the Persian Gulf. When the tides rise, they push river water back upstream, causing the level of the Shatt al Arab to rise.

Vast wetlands once existed along the lower Tigris and Euphrates rivers in southern Iraq. Under Iraqi leader Saddam Hussein (1937–2006), most of these wetlands were drained during the 1990s. The purpose was to drive out people whom Hussein considered political enemies. Hundreds of thousands of Madan people, or Marsh Arabs, lost their homes or were killed by Iraqi military troops. After Hussein lost power in 2003, part of the flow to the wetlands was restored, but much of the marshland had turned to desert.

## Geologic Events

Geologic events have shaped the Tigris and Euphrates basin. Both rivers descend from the Taurus Mountains. Millions of years ago, powerful forces within Earth pushed up thick layers of rock. The layers folded and crumpled, producing the rugged, rocky mountains. The peaks in this region reach heights of more than 11,000 feet (3,350 m).

As water flows down from the Taurus Mountains, it erodes, or wears away, tiny particles of rock and soil. The rivers carry this **sediment** downstream. Where the flow of the rivers slows, the sediment settles

diverts the main flow into the Al Hindiyāh channel, which joins the Tigris at Al Qurnah, forming the Shatt al Arab. Historically, both branches had alternately carried the main flow of the river. Today, the Al Hillah stream flows eastward and does not carry the main flow of the Euphrates.

## The Shatt al Arab

Created by the joining of the Tigris and Euphrates rivers, the Shatt al Arab is a slow-moving river that flows for 120 miles (193 km) before emptying into the Persian Gulf. The amount of water carried by the Tigris and Euphrates rivers affects the level of the Shatt

The dam at Keban, Turkey, is one of several on the Euphrates River.

on the river bottom. When the rivers overflow their banks, silt containing this nutrient-rich sediment settles on the land alongside the banks, making the soil better for growing crops.

## Human Changes

People have made physical changes to the Tigris-Euphrates river system since about 7,000 years ago. At that time, the first canals were built to carry river water to irrigate crops. Since then, both rivers have been altered numerous times.

In Turkey, Syria, and Iraq, engineers have built massive dams to impound, or collect and confine, water as it flows downstream. Once impounded, the water can be carried by canals to crops or drinking-water systems. Dams along the Tigris and Euphrates rivers also help to control floods and are used to generate electricity.

## Natural Resources

In the Tigris-Euphrates basin, the rivers themselves are the most important natural resources. Without their water, life would not be possible in the arid region.

In Iraq, and to a lesser extent in Syria, the region around the Tigris and Euphrates rivers holds rich energy resources. Iraq has more proved oil reserves than any country besides Saudi Arabia, Canada, and Iran. Proved oil reserves are those reserves that have a reasonable certainty of being recoverable.

Oil that is extracted, or removed from the ground, is used to power electricity-generating plants, to heat homes, and to fuel transportation vehicles around the world.

Hasankeyf is an ancient settlement on the Tigris River in southeastern Turkey. The historical site is threatened by Turkey's plans to build a hydroelectric dam nearby.

# Life Along the Rivers

The first people arrived in Mesopotamia in about 10,000 BC. These **nomads**, or wanderers, lived by hunting, fishing, and gathering wild grains and other plants. Eventually, the nomads began to settle in villages. They built houses from clay bricks that were hardened in the sun.

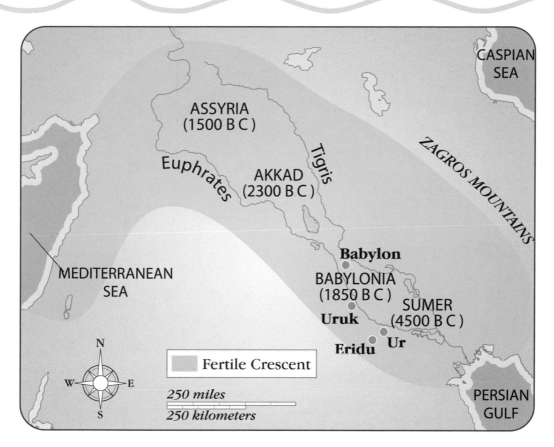

The Fertile Crescent, a semicircular area of rich land around the Tigris and Euphrates rivers and extending to the eastern shore of the Mediterranean Sea, was the site of the ancient civilizations of Sumer, Babylonia, Akkad, and Assyria.

## Early Kingdoms

In about 4500 BC, the first civilization, the kingdom of Sumer, began to develop. Later kingdoms included those of Akkad (2300 BC), Babylonia (1850 BC), and Assyria (1500 BC). Each of these kingdoms was based on agriculture and depended on the waters of the Tigris and Euphrates rivers for growing crops.

## Farming in Mesopotamia

Early Mesopotamian farmers raised pigs, sheep, and goats. They also grew grains such as wheat and barley. Farmers chose the types of grains and other crops that grew best in the local environment. They harvested the seeds and planted them in the rich soil. The Mesopotamian people built canals to carry water from the Tigris and

LEFT: Thousands of years ago, civilizations based on farming grew up along the Tigris and Euphrates rivers.

Euphrates rivers to the fields in order to irrigate crops.

Growing crops and raising animals provided a steady source of food for Mesopotamians. It enabled them to create a **surplus**—a supply of extra food that could be saved for later use. They also traded food with people outside Mesopotamia for resources that did not exist there, such as lumber and stone. Agriculture provided food for the people to trade, and trade brought them wealth.

## Rise of Cities

A steady food supply enabled more people to survive. The population of villages grew. Eventually, villages grew into cities. By 3000 BC, Sumer contained 12 major **city-states**, including Kish, Ur, and Umma. Each city-state had its own government and was independent of the others. A protective brick wall surrounded each city-state for defense from attack. At the center of the city-state was a temple in which the people worshipped many different gods.

## Achievements

Agriculture did more than provide a surplus of food. Because some people did not have to work all the time to grow food, they could work at developing other skills.

By 3500 BC, the Sumerians had invented the wheel. They used wheeled carts to carry goods. Wheels were also used as turntables. Ancient craftspeople used the turntables to make clay pottery for storing food and carrying water. People made tools from wood and copper and wove cloth to fashion clothing.

The people of Mesopotamia were also great builders. Using clay bricks, they built a type of stepped pyramid called a **ziggurat**. The ziggurats were used as temples.

One of the most famous buildings in Mesopotamia was the palace at Babylon. The Hanging Gardens of Babylon, built in about 600 BC, were part of the palace. They were roof gardens laid out on a series of terraces. Water from the Euphrates River was pumped up to the gardens.

## Tools of the Trade

Farmers in ancient Mesopotamia used a tool called a **sickle** to cut grain. A sickle is a long, curved knife. At first, Mesopotamians made sickles from baked clay. Later, they learned to make the blades from copper. Mesopotamians first used wooden plows to **till**, or loosen the soil for planting. Later, they used metal-tipped plows.

Ancient Sumerians created the early writing system known as cuneiform. They pressed wedge-shaped characters into clay tablets.

## Tales on Clay Tablets

By about 4000 BC, Sumerians had begun using reeds to draw on pieces of clay to keep records of supplies and agricultural goods exchanged. This practice led to the development of **cuneiform**, one of the earliest writing systems. The word *cuneiform* means "wedge-shaped." It describes the shape of cuneiform characters. The Sumerians also made a number of important advances in mathematics and in measurement.

Later, the Babylonians developed a numeral system based on the number 60. For this reason, our hour has 60 minutes. Babylonians also used mathematics to predict the movements of the Moon, including eclipses, and they developed calendars based on the **lunar** cycle, the time it takes the Moon to orbit once around Earth. They made advances in medicine, and they were among the first people to use herbal remedies and bandages and to perform minor surgeries.

A portrait of Süleyman the Magnificent, the Ottoman emperor from 1520 to 1566

## Changing Hands

The rich farmland of the region made Mesopotamia a valuable territory. Over thousands of years, a number of different groups used their power to gain control of the area. In 1534 AD, the Ottoman emperor Süleyman took control of much of the Middle East, including present-day Iraq and Syria. The Ottoman Empire had begun

## Hammurabi's Code

Writing enabled Mesopotamians to preserve knowledge and ideas. Hammurabi's Code was one of the first collections of written laws. The code included 282 laws. Among these were rules that governed trade and marriage, as well as punishment for crimes such as theft. Hammurabi was the king of Babylon from 1792 BC to 1750 BC.

This engraving shows Hammurabi receiving the code of laws from Shamash, the god of justice.

in 1302 in what is now Turkey. At its height of power, the empire included much of western Asia, southeastern Europe, and North Africa. It ended in 1922, when the last Ottoman ruler was removed, and the Republic of Turkey was founded in 1923.

During World War I (1914–1918), Ottoman Turkey sided with Germany. Great Britain, France, and other nations fought against Germany and its allies. Great Britain and France supported an Arab rebellion in the Middle East against Ottoman rule. Great Britain took control of Iraq and retained partial control until 1932. In that year, the kingdom of Iraq became an independent nation. Syria gained its independence in 1946 from France, which had taken control in 1920.

Today, the Tigris-Euphrates basin is home to a number of different ethnic groups, including Arabs, Turks, Kurds, and Armenians. The principal religion of the Tigris-Euphrates basin is **Islam**, but people of other religions, including Christians and Jews, live in the region as well.

## Who Was Lawrence of Arabia?

Scholar, soldier, adventurer, and author Thomas Edward Lawrence (1888–1935) was a legendary figure who aided the Arab revolt against the Ottoman Empire during World War I. At that time, the Ottoman Empire, based in Turkey, ruled a large part of the Middle East, including present-day Syria and Iraq, and was allied with Germany in the war. In 1916, with encouragement from Great Britain and France, which were at war with Germany, the Arabs rebelled against the ruling Ottomans. The Arab goals were independence from the Ottoman Empire and the creation of a unified Arab state. Lawrence, a British officer, inspired and led  the Arabs in several successful battles. He wrote an account of the Arab revolt titled *Seven Pillars of Wisdom*, and his exploits were the subject of a famous 1962 film, *Lawrence of Arabia*.

# CHAPTER 4
# Travel and Commerce

Since the earliest centuries of civilization along the Tigris and Euphrates rivers, people have relied on the rivers for transportation and trade. The ancient cities of Mesopotamia are now mere ruins. The central role of the rivers, however, has not diminished.

## An Ancient Trade Network

Ancient Mesopotamia lacked many necessary resources, including stone, lumber, and metals, so the people there traded for those items with people from other regions. The Mesopotamians traded grain, oils, and textiles to people along the Mediterranean Sea and in North Africa.

Early traders traveled on the Tigris and Euphrates rivers in small boats made of wood or reeds. The boats carried cargo such as grain and stones. Not all parts of the rivers were navigable, or able to be traveled by boat, so traders often rode on donkeys or traveled by foot. Over time, trade routes became established, linking the Tigris-Euphrates basin to Europe and to India and other parts of Asia. Trade routes enabled faster, safer travel by traders.

## Modern Trade

Today, land trade dominates in the Tigris-Euphrates basin. Goods are carried by truck and train on routes that extend throughout the region.

Many parts of the Tigris and Euphrates rivers are too shallow to allow passage by large ships, such as

A farmer sorts dates after picking them from palm trees. Dates are a major crop in the Tigris-Euphrates region.

LEFT: A network of trade routes linked Mesopotamia to other parts of the ancient world.

## Goat Boat

One traditional type of boat used in ancient Mesopotamia was the **kalak**. A kalak was a timber raft used for downstream travel. Goatskins filled with air were attached to the underside of the timber, keeping the raft afloat. At the end of a journey, the raft was taken apart, and the timbers were sold. The goatskins were deflated and carried upstream on a donkey to be used for a future trip.

oil tankers and container ships. Much of the trade that takes place on the rivers is done using **shallow-draft vessels**. Because these boats ride high in the water, they can travel where the rivers are not very deep. On the Tigris River, vessels can navigate as far upstream as the Iraqi city of Mosul. On the Euphrates, boats can travel upstream to the Iraqi city of Hit.

## Agriculture Today

Irrigation is as important to the farmers of the Tigris and Euphrates region today as it was to the ancient Mesopotamians. In many places along the rivers, huge dams contain water for use in agricultural irrigation systems. Among the largest dams are the Ataturk Dam in southeastern Turkey, the Euphrates Dam in north-central Syria, and the Mosul Dam in northern Iraq. Canals, pumps, and pipelines deliver irrigation water to crops in the fields and supply water for livestock. Some of the region's major crops are dates, wheat, barley, and cotton.

The land around the Shatt al Arab is a significant area for agriculture. Among the major crops grown there are dates and rice. Crops are irrigated naturally when tides from the Persian Gulf come in and raise the water level of the Shatt al Arab.

## Commerce on the Persian Gulf

Basra is Iraq's chief port, or place where ships load and unload. It is

**FAST FACT**
In 2008, the United States imported an average of 627,000 barrels of oil per day from Iraq.

A huge tanker docks at an oil terminal in the Persian Gulf.

## Salt Assault

Years of irrigation can seriously damage soil. **Salinization**, or the buildup of salt, takes place when irrigation water that contains salt, evaporates into the air or when plants absorb it through their roots. The salt, which does not evaporate and which plants do not use, remains. The salt content of the soil increases. Severe salinization makes the soil unsuitable for growing crops.

located on the Shatt al Arab, about 70 miles (110 km) upstream from the Persian Gulf. Basra is also the center of Iraq's **petroleum refining** industry. At refineries, crude oil is manufactured into finished petroleum products. Finished products made from petroleum include gasoline, diesel fuel, jet fuel, heating oil, and kerosene. Products from the refineries are then shipped by pipeline to Al Faw, an Iraqi city on the Persian Gulf. There, they are loaded onto large ships called supertankers for transport to countries around the world.

# CHAPTER 5

# An Uncertain Future

Today, millions of people in Turkey, Syria, and Iraq depend on the Tigris and Euphrates rivers to survive. Without the rivers, the people of the region would not have water to drink, to irrigate crops, or to raise livestock. But the amount of water is limited. As the populations in the Tigris-Euphrates basin grow, so do the demands for water—and the conflicts that result. The three nations have not always agreed on how much water should be allotted for each population. To date, the disagreements have been mostly peaceful. The threat of "water wars," however, is always present.

The Ataturk Dam, on the Euphrates River in southeastern Turkey, supplies Syria and Iraq with a large part of their water supply. Disputes have occurred between Turkey and its downstream neighbors regarding water supply.

## Learning to Share

Since 1964, Turkey, Syria, and Iraq have worked to negotiate agreements about water use. Officials have tried to calculate how much water each country needs. They have worked to ensure that each country gets the needed amount. Despite these efforts, the countries have been unable to agree on how much water each nation needs and how to divide the water fairly. Twice, in 1975 and 1998, war almost broke out as a result of these disagreements.

In 1987, Turkey and Syria reached an agreement that Turkey would release about 50 percent of the water of the Euphrates River downstream to Syria. In 1990, Syria and Iraq also reached an agreement. Syria would send 52 percent of the Euphrates River's flow it received from Turkey downstream to Iraq. But Turkey's work on a large-scale dam development project raised concerns about the availability of water in countries farther downstream.

## Dams and Demand

In the 1970s, Turkey began the $32 billion Southeastern Anatolia

LEFT: A woman inspects the arid soil of her land near Baghdad, Iraq. Below-average rainfall and low water levels in the Euphrates and Tigris rivers have left parts of Iraq bone-dry in recent years.

Turkey, Syria, and Iraq have built numerous dams on the Tigris and Euphrates rivers for both agricultural irrigation and hydroelectric power.

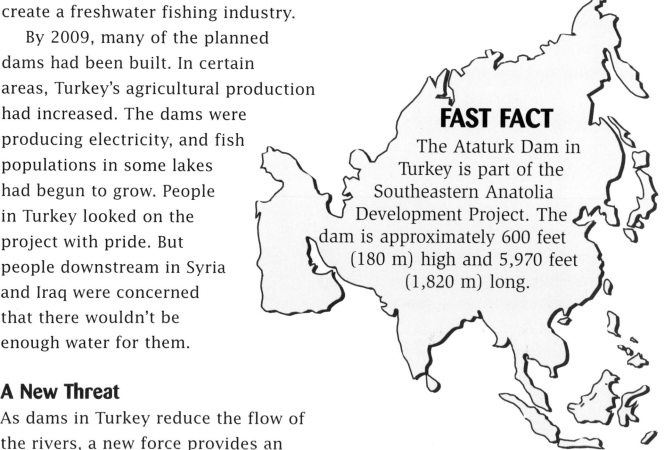

Development Project. Turkey planned to build 22 dams on the Tigris and Euphrates rivers. The dams would provide irrigation for farming. They would also produce hydroelectric power for use by people in Turkey. In addition, the lakes formed by the dams would be stocked with fish. Turkey hoped to create a freshwater fishing industry.

By 2009, many of the planned dams had been built. In certain areas, Turkey's agricultural production had increased. The dams were producing electricity, and fish populations in some lakes had begun to grow. People in Turkey looked on the project with pride. But people downstream in Syria and Iraq were concerned that there wouldn't be enough water for them.

## A New Threat

As dams in Turkey reduce the flow of the rivers, a new force provides an

**FAST FACT**
The Ataturk Dam in Turkey is part of the Southeastern Anatolia Development Project. The dam is approximately 600 feet (180 m) high and 5,970 feet (1,820 m) long.

even greater threat to people downstream. Shifting weather patterns, perhaps influenced by global climate change, may increase pressure on the water supply. In 2008 and 2009, severe **drought**, or lack of rainfall, struck the region. The water flowing from Turkish dams slowed to a trickle. Across Syria and Iraq, crops withered and died.

## Hope for the Future

In 2008, Turkey, Syria, and Iraq established a water institute to work on water-related problems among the three nations. It is hoped that more international cooperation will enable the region's water supplies to meet people's needs—and that life in the Tigris-Euphrates basin will go on, as it has for thousands of years.

Residents collect water from a stream near Baghdad, Iraq. Iraqis say Turkey's dams have reduced the flow of the Tigris and Euphrates rivers, worsening the water shortage caused by drought conditions in the Middle East.

NOTABLE QUOTE

*"The ancient Fertile Crescent will disappear in this century."*

—Akio Kitoh, director of the Climate Research department of Japan's Meteorological Research Institute

# COMPARING THE WORLD'S RIVERS

| River | Continent | Source | Outflow | Approximate Length in miles (kilometers) | Area of Drainage Basin in square miles (square kilometers) |
|---|---|---|---|---|---|
| Amazon | South America | Andes Mountains, Peru | Atlantic Ocean | 4,000 (6,450) | 2.7 million (7 million) |
| Euphrates | Asia | Murat and Kara Su rivers, Turkey | Persian Gulf | 1,740 (2,800) | 171,430 (444,000) |
| Ganges | Asia | Himalayas, India | Bay of Bengal | 1,560 (2,510) | 400,000 (1 million) |
| Mississippi | North America | Lake Itasca, Minnesota | Gulf of Mexico | 2,350 (3,780) | 1.2 million (3.1 million) |
| Nile | Africa | Streams flowing into Lake Victoria, East Africa | Mediterranean Sea | 4,145 (6,670) | 1.3 million (3.3 million) |
| Rhine | Europe | Alps, Switzerland | North Sea | 865 (1,390) | 65,600 (170,000) |
| St. Lawrence | North America | Lake Ontario, Canada and United States | Gulf of St. Lawrence | 744 (1,190) | 502,000 (1.3 million) |
| Tigris | Asia | Lake Hazar, Taurus Mountains, Turkey | Persian Gulf | 1,180 (1,900) | 43,000 (111,000) |
| Yangtze | Asia | Damqu River, Tanggula Mountains, China | East China Sea | 3,915 (6,300) | 690,000 (1.8 million) |

# TIMELINE

| | |
|---|---|
| **10,000 BC** | People have settled in the Tigris-Euphrates basin. |
| **5000 BC** | People build the first irrigation canals on the Tigris and Euphrates rivers. |
| **4500 BC** | The kingdom of Sumer arises. |
| **4000 BC** | Sumerians develop a writing system to record information on clay tablets. |
| **3500 BC** | Sumerians have invented the wheel. |
| **3000 BC** | Sumer includes 12 major cities. |
| **2150 BC** | Akkad and Sumer are constantly at war. |
| **1850 BC** | The city of Babylon gains control of much of Mesopotamia. |
| **1500 BC** | The kingdom of Assyria begins its rise as a great empire. |
| **1534** | Ottomans control Iraq and Syria. |
| **1916** | Supported by Great Britain and France, Arabs in Syria, Iraq, and elsewhere in the Middle East begin a revolt against Ottoman rule. |
| **1918** | Great Britain controls Iraq. |
| **1923** | The Republic of Turkey is established. |
| **1932** | Iraq becomes an independent nation. |
| **1946** | Syria gains independence from France. |
| **1970s** | Turkey begins the Southeastern Anatolia Development Project, with plans to build 22 dams on the Tigris and Euphrates rivers. |
| **1987** | Turkey and Syria reach a water-sharing agreement. |
| **1990** | Syria and Iraq reach a water-sharing agreement. |
| **2008–2009** | Severe drought strikes the Tigris-Euphrates basin. |

# GLOSSARY

**alluvial plain** A flat landform created by deposits of sediment over time by one or more rivers

**canals** Human-made waterways that are used for shipping or irrigation

**city-states** A self-governing political unit made up of a city and the surrounding territory

**cuneiform** A writing system using wedge-shaped characters

**drainage basin** The area of land drained by a river and its tributaries

**drought** A long period of little or no rainfall

**embankments** Raised structures (usually of earth or gravel) used to hold back water

**Fertile Crescent** A semicircle of fertile land in the Middle East stretching from the eastern shore of the Mediterranean Sea to the Persian Gulf

**generator** A machine that makes electricity

**gorges** Narrow canyons with steep walls

**hydroelectricity** Electricity that is produced by the power of moving water

**irrigation** The watering of land in an artificial way to foster plant growth

**Islam** The religious faith of Muslims, including belief in Allah and in the teachings of the prophet Muhammed

**kalak** A traditional Asian boat for downstream transportation on rivers

**limestone** A type of rock that is formed from the shell remains of sea animals and that is used as a building material

**lunar** Having to do with the Moon

**nomads** People who move from place to place, usually seasonally and within a certain territory

**petroleum refining** The process by which crude oil is made into finished petroleum products

**plateau** A broad, flat area of high land

**reservoir** An artificial lake in which water is collected and kept for use

**salinization** The buildup of salts—for example, in soil

**sediment** Material deposited by water, wind, or glaciers

**shallow-draft vessels** Boats that ride high in the water and are able to navigate shallow waterways

**sickle** A farming tool with a curved blade attached to a short handle, used for cutting grain or tall grass

**silt** Small particles of sand or rock left as sediment

**surplus** The amount of something that remains after the immediate need is satisfied

**till** To prepare land for raising crops

**tributaries** Smaller rivers and streams that flow into larger bodies of water

**turbine** A machine powered by rotating blades

**ziggurat** An ancient Mesopotamian temple structure with stepped levels

# FIND OUT MORE

## BOOKS

Apte, Sunita. *Mesopotamia*. Children's Press, 2009.

Mountjoy, Shane. *The Tigris and Euphrates*. Facts on File, 2005.

Schomp, Virginia. *Ancient Mesopotamia: The Sumerians, Babylonians, and Assyrians*. Children's Press, 2005

Somervill, Barbara A. *Empires of Ancient Mesopotamia*. Chelsea House Publishers, 2009.

Steele, Phillip, and John Farndon. *Mesopotamia*. DK Children, 2007.

Mehta-Jones, Shilpa. *Life in Ancient Mesopotamia*. Crabtree Publishing Company, 2005

## WEB SITES

**The British Museum: Mesopotamia**
www.mesopotamia.co.uk/menu.html

**National Geographic Kids: Iraq**
http://kids.nationalgeographic.com/Places/Find/Iraq

**Social Studies for Kids: Ancient Middle East**
www.socialstudiesforkids.com/subjects/ancientmiddleeast.htm

## ABOUT THE AUTHOR

Gary Miller is a writer and documentary filmmaker. He has written about everything from burrowing owls to gorillas, and wireless technology to wild wolves. Gary has interviewed country music stars, stock car racers, stunt plane fliers, civil rights pioneers, and rocket scientists. When he's not writing or working on a movie, he can often be found kayaking or fly fishing on the rivers of Vermont.

# INDEX

Page references in **bold** type are to illustrations.